BODILY PRESENCE

BODILY PRESENCE

BY

BLAINE MARCHAND

QUARRY PRESS

cOnteNTS

DiscOveRinG BuoYanCy

BodiLY PreSeNcE

Bodily Presence

I

Taken with my Brownee Instamatic
that overcast April day,
Paul, my best friend,
and I are out-of-focus.
Our six-year old bodies
like little old men
in the stiff wool jackets
and heavy grey flannels
worn to our First Communion.
On my left arm,
the gold tassled satin ribbon
that was kept in a beige box
beneath the window seat
of my parent's bedroom,
a treasure to be passed
from son to son for the occasion.
Our hands are weights
as we lean away from each other,
already pulling apart,
just as we would do, despite years
of shared secrets.

In the next snap,
my mother
in her tailored coat,
the hat with a long narrow feather.
How I remember
the nap of the coat pressing
against the cleaner's bag
as if it were suffocating,
the creases in the arms,
sinews of muscles
straining to get out.
And the hat, a stuffed bird nesting
in the tissue paper of the hat box
in the tiny clothes closet.
She stands at a distance,

hands buried in her coat pockets,
looks off to the left
as if in thought,
perhaps the demands
of eight children
and a sickly husband
troubling her.

And then one of me
alone. I seem engulfed
by the frame of the large front porch
with its massive squared columns.
At my back
the door is shut.
In this one
I scowl with worry.

And then the last —
of my father and me,
a surprising one.
It isn't his elegance
that I always recall,
even the way
the fingers of his left hand cradled
the ivory cigarette holder.
It is his right hand
resting on my shoulder,
with the lightness of a bird.
The smile on his face,
as if he were indeed
proud of me.

2

We tuck our legs under ourselves,
fold our hands into our laps
as Sister Imelda tells us,
huddle on the floor
around the hem of her brown habit,
like the picture of Jesus on the wall,
the one that says
Gather Unto Me Little Children,
the one I now proudly can read,
though I catch myself,
pride is a sin.
Sister strokes the silver crucifix
that hangs from a black rope
around her neck, clears her throat.

"These are the most important
days of your lives.
They will mark you forever.
Making a First Confession takes
your sins away;
you can receive First Communion,
the Bodily Presence of Jesus.
At Confirmation when the Bishop
makes you soldiers of Christ,
he gives you the new name you have chosen.
A name is a sign you carry to death.
You must think deeply about it,
as I did when I entered the convent.
Imelda... it is unusual."
She pulls her veil, hides her cheek
as she blushes. "Listen carefully."
She claps her hands, we are restless.
"Blessed Imelda entered the convent, yet
had not reached the age of reason,
could not make her First Confession."

Sister holds her head high,
looks up the through the window
to the peaked silver roof of the church.

It skewers the sun, hurts your eyes
if you look at it too long,
like the Host will if you stare
when Jesus enters it during Mass.
 "One day Blessed Imelda fell ill,
the Sisters knew she would not live.
Because she was so young and so holy,
she could not have sinned,
the Sisters hurried to the Bishop,
begged him to give her Communion."

Her small white hands flutter wide,
one drops, straightens a pleat
fallen open, errant over her knees.
 "The Bishop brought the Sacred Host
and placed it above her heart."
Her finger, the one with the silver ring,
circles the very spot.
 "Praise be to God, a miracle —
the Host disappeared into her body
just as Blessed Imelda took her last breath."
She crosses herself, draws a white hanky,
daubs her eyes softly. Not one of us stirs.
At recess, in the corner of the schoolyard,
far removed from the door she guards,
we boys leave off our games.
Some scoff, in the way adults often do.
Others reason:
names must be chosen carefully.

3

"I've committed murder."
"Ya, well I've committed adultery."
"You don't even know what it means!"
Paul shoves me.
The brown spears of radiator dig in my back.
"Do too!"
The black edge of my running shoe
misses his shin, the hollow tube
of heating coil groans.
Sister rises in the pew like a bird of prey,
genuflects quickly, as she taught us not to do.
The curtain of the confession billows
as a classmate blurs by; Paul slips in.
The leather of the kneeler wheezes with his weight.
The black beads, like tight knots, in Sister's hands
lash her starched habit. She stands
directly opposite me,
but I stare at the granite floor.
I join my hands in prayer,
raise them to my lips, close my eyes.
I go down the list she has given us,
the way my mother does before we go shopping.
I took God's name in vain once,
I lied twice, I disobeyed my parents three times."

The confessional window slides shut,
a classmate's feet scurry down the aisle.
I escape into the cold dark space, kneel.
"I stole candy four times."
I think of the tricks we are learning
in arithmetic — addition, subtraction,
and the diagram in our catechism,
the milk bottle to explain our souls,
so white and pure,
how sins make it dark and darker.
Sister says this is bad, but it always reminds me
of chocolate milk, which I love,
which our mother only allows on special occasions.

The wicket door slides open and Father Kennedy's face
is a shadow beyond the window veil.
His hand crosses the air,
he mumbles something I cannot hear.
I clear my throat. "Bless me Father,
for I have sinned, I have never... ."
I start to shake, I have forgotten the words.
Outside the curtain Sister's shoes scrape,
the rosary clicks through her fingernails.
"Begin again," he coaxes me,
and out the sins I have memorized come
in a long line like my tin Crusaders
I place on the shelves
of the desk in the hall at home
as I prepare them to go into battle,
storming the castle,
defeating the Infidel.

4

The fire alarm box —
red as the heart of Jesus
we pray will save us —
is on the telephone post above
the head of my older brother
as I pace back and forth,
my hands bristling
my brushcut into place.
I don't know why we're waiting
here at the corner —
except my father had not come home from the office,
had not called and my mother was frightened,
tapping her foot, straightening
things in the kitchen,
and my brother and I dressed for church,
for my First Communion.
I don't know why she has sent us ahead.
I told her over and over
Sister Imelda had given strict instructions
to arrive as a family and in plenty of time.
I look at my watch. Finally
my older brother says we'll go ahead.
I start to say
"Sister Imelda said",
but he reached his age of reason four years ago.
I struggle to match his stride,
check over my shoulder now and again,
hope my parents are coming.

Sister Imelda gives me that look,
the way the old parrot down the street
angles its head. I am always afraid
with its sharp beak it will swoop down.
I forget my place in line,
slip in among the taller boys,
next to Paul.
Sister grabs my arm. The white satin ribbon
my mother had perfectly tied
falls to the ground, lies there
like a white dove I once saw crushed

on the road. "Look what you've done!"
She picks up the ribbon, fastens it;
it straggles loosely.
"Disobedient thing!" She hauls me out,
down the line into place
opposite Karen, who, like me, is blonde and short.
"Everything must balance."

From the depths of her pockets she pulls out
holy pictures the size of the hockey cards
we play keepsy with all winter.
I wedge mine between my upraised fingers,
hope she will be pleased.
On the back, in her careful printing,
my name and the date;
on the front, an angel —
one hand on a boy's shoulder,
the other pointing, guiding him forward.
Sister straightens her teabrown habit,
clacks the wooden clapper twice
and the separate lines of boys and girls
file through the school door,
across the yard and up
the flight of stairs people sometimes
climb on their knees.
"Your souls," she sings,
"shiny as your new shoes."

The doors of the church are pulled wide,
like the folds of Jesus' robe
in the picture of the Sacred Heart.
And there, at the centre,
is the sanctuary lamp.
Sister tells us it is a sign.
Behind the white cloth
on the tabernacle
Jesus, who sees every bad thing
we do, is present.

The lamp pulses red as blood,
like the flashing light at the busy corner
warning me if I cross I will be killed.
How can I receive him?
I stiffen, finger the ribbon
Sister retied. I have sinned.

6

High up on the altar,
in a wooden chair, the Bishop
waits for me.
At the ends of its arms
lions' mouths are open,
each leg a paw with claws.
To his left, on the large cross,
blood drips down the wounds on the body of Jesus;
to his right, amid the martyrs,
is St. George in armour,
a spear thrust into the mouth
of a dragon I know is really the devil.
He waits for me in the dark alley
between two garages I must pass
on my way home from school
in winter when it is dark.
I run as fast as I can,
hold my breath because my oldest brother
told me the devil can enter me through the air.
Then I will become demon seed.
God will banish me
to the fires of Hell forever.

The Bishop, wearing robes of white,
clutches a golden staff
with a gloved hand.
His other, the one with the ring
that Sister told us is embedded
with a piece of the True Cross
Jesus died on for our sins,
rests in his lap waiting
to slap me on the cheek,
make me a soldier of Christ.
I must be prepared
to give up my life
for Him.

My eldest sister, already finished school,
stands beside me as my witness.
She is wearing a mauve dress
that reminds me of the lilacs
on the hedge in our yard
we escape to when we play run-chief-run.
Her crinoline crinkles just like leaves
when she moves. The sound comforts me.
I have chosen the name Joseph.
Because my two brothers have
and neither have died.
Because he was the father of Jesus
and Sister told us he was beloved by God
and lived a long life.

7

Although the green leather seats are cracked,
patched with a cross-stitch of tape,
although it is not really a bus
as its front pretends,
it is the place I select
when my parents say
our family will go out
after the ceremony,
something we never do.
It is my favourite
because my three sisters
bring me here
each Sunday after 8:30 Mass.
I love how they swing me
between them in the air
while we wait
for the street light to change
so we can safely cross and enter.
Because of the waitress with a small comb in her hair,
like the wafer she tucks into ice cream sundaes.
Because of her smile as she brings me
the hot chocolate and toast
without having to order.
Today, it is the presents
like building blocks
in bright coloured paper
which I open slowly, delay the surprise,
keeping to last the one from my oldest sister —
a rosary, its beads bright as the glass
around the candle my mother
lights to remember the dead after Mass,
and a prayer book in stitched red leather,
on the inside the date in gold.
But best of all, today, everyone is here,
and I am in the centre
with my two older brothers on each side,
then my three sisters, my parents
— even my father who is laughing
as my two little brothers

slip off and on the chairs,
toddle up and down the aisle,
spinning stools as they giggle,
explore this place they have never
been to, but that I allow them
because being six
I have reached the age of reason
and can now choose.

tHe LOok On My MotHer's fACe

The Look on My Mother's Face

"What's bugging you?"
my fourteen year-old son demands.
My head jerks in response,
pulls me out of
a blank space where I often retreat.
A space where nothing exists
but a low hum, like the one
that once went through my body
when I put my hand into the back
of the television set
trying to stop the repeating image.

"It's the way you purse your lips
and tilt your head.
The way your eyes go blank."
I smile, then laugh.
How can I explain
that sometimes things
weigh me down,
lead hidden in the hem of curtains
so they hang straight,
won't blow open.

I understand his concern.
Recently I saw a photograph
of my mother and me
on my First Communion Day.
There was that look on her face:
the head to one side,
the lips locked in a grimace,
the eyes in another dimension.
I too began to question why.
Was it something I had said or done?
Or fatigue, such a large family
and my father not well?

But then I began to wonder.
Was hers the same secret I keep hidden?
That first time I learned to do it —

my mind retreating, distancing itself
from the dark stranger in the woods
towering over me,
his rough hands
parting and stroking the surge of my body.

Baby Mice

Look, he said,
prying
the metal back
as if it were
the mouth of a monster.

Inside the fender
of the rusty thrasher
abandoned
in the woods,
a nest.

Baby mice.
White as teeth.

Square hand reached
down.
Thumb and forefinger,
a stalking cat,
pinched one
took it out,
laid it on the boy's palm.

Thick fingers stroked
the hairless thing
that raised its head,
cradled its mouth
against the mount of flesh.

Fingers lifted it,
set it back
among the other bodies,
wriggling like worms.

Look, he said,
and moved closer to the boy.

Thumb and forefinger,
as if clenched teeth,
yanked the clasp of zipper.

The boy's eyes caught
the wind in the branches
of pines overhead.

The scent, the sound invading
the pores of his body
as it seemed to rise
then suddenly
fall in a heap.

Look, he said,
as he ripped
bark from a small cedar log.

Look
as the rotting lid cracked open.

Look
as the jagged end thrust down

the sounds of
squashing bones and mews rose
out of its throat.

The Flaw

It still disturbs me
— the furnace's low rumble
that shook me from sleep.
A month ago, pursued by a nightmare,
I woke, heard the air trapped
in the radiators crack,
small bones in large hands.
I rushed down into the cold basement,
found smoke curdling into the air.
Even though the repairman later reasoned
it was only a minor flaw, the burner would have shut off,
the smoke, the loud whine of that morning haunt me.

Funny how his words were no balm.
Like those offered thirty years ago by the priest,
at the end of the bed, in a rasping voice:
"I don't know what made me do it.
Will you pretend it never happened?
Can you forgive me as God will?"
All the while
I refused to look up at him,
saw only the stub of cigarette
in his fingers, its redness a scar
left by a burn; heard his palm coax
the stubble of his beard into compliance,
its sound what my throat would not shape.

He, the one who had taught me
the closeness of love.
But that was innocent.
We would sit in the shade of the balcony,
laugh and talk of spiritual things.
Until one day I complained about the heat.
He suggested a short nap.
I lay down. His hand slid into my pants.
The sun streamed through the window,
its warmth lulling me to sleep.

I awoke to his dark form,
a cloud blotting the sun,
smoke seeping from his nostrils.
I learned love is dangerous.
A furnace.

The Story of a Soul *

And they sang so sweetly after his sermon,
Te Deum filling the chapel
the way migrating birds chant
in the apple trees of the cloister
when an autumn day is blessed as summer.
Their knees almost seemed to rise
from the *priedieux* as they spread
their arms wide, rapturous with love.
He had held out an example,
St. Theresa of the Child Jesus,
her simple way,
recalling her words:
"To pick up a pin for love
can convert a soul."
Then her death,
fearing deprivation
of the light of faith,
yet repeating:
"I would not suffer less."
And as if it were a miracle,
a shaft of sun pierced the windows
and the nuns translucent
as the tapers on the altar,
their voices hovering
with the wisps of smoke
and incense rising to the frescoes
smiling down upon them.

But later, to me, as I drew away,
he spoke of the Circumcision of Jesus.
His hand sliding
to the button at my waist.
I wanted to run.
But my body was bursting,
as if I were walking home
past the dark alley,
flames of fear erupting
along the curve of my spine.

I wanted to run
but I let his arms take me,
the way bars hold a bird
(and yet it still sings).

(*title of the spiritual autobiography of St. Theresa Liseux)

Graduation

I could not tell the truth
after my friends from the public school
oo-ed and ah-ed when I told them
my graduating class was going to Montreal.
How could I explain the reason was to visit
a shrine where men and women joyfully
did penance on their knees,
cleansed their souls
by climbing the endless flight
of cement stairs leading to the Oratory?

They would never understand
the crutches, the braces, the canes
hanging in columns on the walls,
nor the scrawled notes,
testifying to the afflictions,
the claims to have been cured.

Nor the flaccid heart of Brother Andre,
floating in formaldehyde,
behind ruby glass
in the wall. A relic
of a simple man who denied
s every need,
k up any menial task
omplish his dream
a church to the husband
gin Mary.

How could I say
I needed to believe
to boys who smoked and scratched their groins
while craving endlessly for girls;
needed to believe
in the sermon on the mount,
that "blessed are the meek",
to hold back the schism
created in me by a man
who gave me the Body of Christ
each morning, and his own body,
but only when he chose?

A Smooth Face

Each morning my mother insisted:
wash your face.
Having scrubbed it the night before;
how, I wondered, could it be dirty?
Half-heartedly, I would linger
closing my eyes and slip
into the ebbing sensations
of my recurring dream:
flying home from school,
body swooping through low-lying mist,
arms and legs brushed by soft tips of pine.

Father Aloysius, always pushed
his large crucifix further down
behind the cincture at his pencil-thin waist
when he talked of idle hands and thoughts,
spoke of concupiscence. At fourteen,
I did not understand; but at lunch,
hidden among the library stacks,
away from prying eyes,
I fumbled through a dictionary.

How well I've learned my lessons.
Each morning, soap lathers and the sharp edge
of a razor shears stubble from my chin.
A smooth face ready to begin another day
of budgets, employees and clients,
poised above a dry-cleaned suit
reflecting the reserve of my voice and hands.

How do we break through?
In life we are taught to cover up,
words and actions barriers.
Why can't we peel away the layers,
admit to the secret selves
we tuck away into dreams.
It should be easy.

The way my mother,
with a kitchen knife,
uncurled the skin of apples,
laid wedges of the fleshy pulp
in a diminishing spiral
in the pies she served each Sunday;
the way Father Aloysius had
when he returned to class from lunch,
the pungence of oranges
springing from his fingers
without his ever noticing it
as he leaned close,
his pen checking the equations
I had copied into my notebook.

The Well

They believed
it was a sign.
When people gathered
on the steps after Sunday mass
they repeated
how the priest's body
was found at twilight
floating,
arms spread out
as if crucified,
his cassock rippling
on the water,
a dark clot of weeds,
threaded through his fingers,
a rosary, brown as the cattails
that choked the bank.
They spread word
of his piety,
recounted how he came there,
far from the church,
beyond the tangle
of tombstones and grass,
prayed for salvation
by the creek
on hot summer evenings
craving relief.
It was an act of God,
they were certain
and raised funds
to build a holy well.

For eighty years
people have come
from far-flung places
to drink the water,
petition for cures,
seek favours from
Our Lady of Perpetual Help
who clutching her Son,
looks down on them
through arrangements
of artificial flowers.

Over the years
they have left
only their names
in a ledger,
their pain kept
private,
ever hopeful.
One begs:
"Please.
I love him so much.
Let him return.
In the name of God."

Obituary

Yes, I suppose this is how it should be
after two decades of silence.
The last words, newspaper copy:
baptismal names; birthdate; age;
parents' names; brothers', sisters';
date of ordination;
place and time of memorial mass.
Your life, a litany.
But there was so much more,
so much mystery
that I can no longer accept
what I did as an obedient child
told it was an act of faith.

Questions, like catechism,
trespass in unguarded moments,
mingle with memories of the forbidden,
the pleasures you taught me
in your rituals of religion and sex,
(pleasures I hide in my heart,
a fragment of bone in a reliquary),
and, after each time,
your confession whispered
— remorse, guilt, renunciation —
emotions I was too young to understand,
now reconciled through the passage of years.

All settled under my skin
on the day you told me never to come again —
the sharp edge of your voice
driving into my flesh;
the salty wetness of your handkerchief
stinging my face.

*i*MprinT

This Divided House

Who lives on the other side of this divided house?
Each morning, the daily ritual:
pad of footsteps, grind of chair against floor,
thud of cupboard, rattle of cup and saucer.
The pleading of a telephone,
click of machine, a muffled voice
begging a message.

We all ask this about ourselves.
Who is the real person living inside?
Not the one who goes about tasks,
mindless as a wind-up toy;
not the one parents, teachers, bosses
shape by offering some reward;
not the one we assume to please lovers.
But the other filling the inside
of the head with arguments
that boil the blood,
promising, *next time, next time*.

On the other side of the wall,
something shatters.
A bottle hitting the floor
and the air, for an instant,
liquid with milk.
The body when it finally lets go,
semen shooting, streaking the fingers.
Image of thighs or a haired chest
fading from the mind
as eyes, pinched tight, open
to sharp light, pinpoints of pleasure
subsiding from the knees —

A man lying alone amid cold sheets thrown back,
suddenly empty as the other side of the double bed,
longing to hold onto flesh;
but determined to get the day going
with the tannic of tea,
the solitary ways of lessening pain.

Disparate Things

You lie so still beside me,
breathing hushed as a folding swan's wing,
your hand curved, like its neck, about my thigh.
Who knows what world you have entered,
plunging into a dreamscape
driven by instinct, by appetite,
navigating like an eel past reeds that reach out,
threaten to entangle, drown you.

Awake, I am alone,
reluctant to give up the sheer pleasure,
floating on the billow of climax
ebbing in my veins.
I take in the things around my room:
jagged lip of wooden bowl;
smooth handle of Greek pottery;
the way the shower of sunlight floods them,
two disparate things made one.

Imprint

Flux of temperature, smattering of snow
break the clutch of frost
that has coated this city.
New Year's Day.
A neighbour puts her sons out
in the yard to play.
They are bundled, protected
against the biting elements.
Knowing she is never far away,
they push each other, stand up, examine
their bodies' imprints in the powder
layered across the frozen garden.
From the kitchen window she watches
as she washes up lunch's debris.

Although a new year has begun
Joni Mitchell's plaintive lyrics about passing love
fill the dusty apartment with pain.
My son has chosen to stay overnight at a friend's
in that ritual of teenage male bonding.
And you are on a bus to Montreal,
plugged into your Walkman,
swaying to Sting's anthem about imprisonment.
On the bus, taking you to your ex-lover
and the city of his birth.
He wants you but you want me
and I still grieve for my wife.

As you watch from your seat
the city's towers grow large against
the wintry thigh of Mount Royal.
As I watch from my bedroom window
one boy slips into the house.
The other, suddenly aware his sibling has gone,
begins to cry. With him I plead
to be allowed in.

Preserve

We do not need to talk.
There is the sound of our boots
sinking through snow
along this path
others before us have taken.
And the air, rich with the sounds
of the river, a burnished grey,
a sluice of silver, as it crystallizes
a vein of rock piercing its current.
And above the sky, lapis lazuli,
striations of cloud, and the sun
on our faces, warm as our hands
last night when we made love.

In the distance, the dark
concentration of the city,
an ominous baroque pearl.

But for now we turn away.

From the outstretched limbs of trees
swoop crested cardinals,
tufts red as the berries
on the nearby bush.
The birds gather and drink
from the open gash of water,
flit back to their perches.

You turn and I follow.
My boots sink deep into unbroken snow
as we wander into the heart
of the woods. A wind shudders
the burgundy candles of sumach,
the mahogany canes of dogwood.

We do not speak.
No need.
This preserve is our reserve.

Craving

If only it were as simple
as the body's craving,
smooth as the limbs
of lovers, their hands
spilling over,
their mouths
a profusion of kisses
and promises.

But it never is. There's always
the fear. Inevitable as
the way the two, exhausted,
lie apart until the cold
current of air leaking through
the open window drives them
to hide under blankets
or rise
and get dressed.

Sure, there are the motions —
fingers link, arms entwine,
eyes cannot get enough;
the reassurances, bright
as the lamp in the hall.
But on the stairs
the pair of departing feet echo,
loud as the isolation
nagging at the other's heart.

Silent partners

Why should it be this way?
You and I, one day compliant
as February under warm southern winds,
hard snow giving itself up
to the strengthening sun;
the next day so bitter,
raw chill that turns
everything rigid,
lacerates any skin that is exposed.
And then the inevitable poems
where all is carefully altered
— camouflaged behind metaphors,
given voice through some vague persona
that we discuss and reshape
safely over the phone.

Let's be honest.
Do away with the intrigue, the artifice.
Each of us brings a queue of silent partners.
You, the parents who caught you
in their vice of anger and hurt,
squeezed you until, bent to their shape,
you fled to lovers who left
time and time again.
And I, those years of watching
my wife slowly die
— one death in a series,
always left behind,
holding pain inside,
a snared, clawing, wild bird,
and yes, the simple fear
of loving men,
those rough hands
that took me, as a child,
into the decaying autumn woods
and the priest
whose stubble bruised my face
as he frisked my pubescent body
for a semblance of love.

The Cracks

The photo on the March leaf
of the calendar
is a gardener's delight. Yet
outside flux
between thaw and freeze
ruts the sidewalks, roads,
renders them treacherous.
The emptied dining and living rooms
of this apartment
echo. Footsteps.
Noise in a shell.
Twenty years of possessions
piled high in a bedroom
because the ceilings
have cracked.
Webs of flaking paint,
debris on the floor.
Will repair merely hide
the faults? Will they
continue to spread
beneath the false cover?

At the next corner,
Byron and Clarendon,
a city worker in the limbs
of the last surviving elm
along the ribbon of park.
In his hands, a saw
fells branch after branch
because this tree,
in last summer's drought,
needing water, drove
its roots through
the cellar of the nearby house,
unsettled its foundation,
floors and walls.

The phone rings and rings.
It is your voice
from the other side of the country where
everything is already
in bloom. You say
I sound hurried, pressed.
My suitcase lies open,
waiting for out-of-season things
to be packed
for my flight
across the equator, into Africa.
Your voice, elusive as fog,
groggy with early morning,
makes me want your arms.
To still, at least
for a moment,
my fatalism,
unrelenting as the chainsaw,
pervasive as cracks in plaster.

Case After Case

This spring season is unsettling.
Winter tenacious, not letting go.
The atmosphere full of disturbance -
snow pelting the facades of houses,
drizzling to rain that clogs
the streets and gutters with slush.
All the trees still frozen in ice
that last night congealed against the windows.

Why in life do we also refuse to let go?
Whether a patient in the cancer ward,
body growing thin, eyes large
with the terror of what approaches,
the nurse at the door with a tray of needles
to take yet more blood;
or a lover, who calls and cries
at the hurt he has caused you and the pain he now feels,
searching for an answer neither has;
or me, looking across the table
at his face distraught above espresso and pie,
my heart still wanting to comfort him.

Once in a Harvard museum,
I saw flowers sculpted from glass.
Even after one hundred years,
their botanical execution so exact
they could be used for study.
But no. They were always too fragile,
had to be locked away, in case after case,
from the awkward handling of humans.

Narcotic

After words, harsh as stone against stone,
we find solace in each other's body,
earth under rain,
the stalks of spring bulbs
growing heavy and full.
The chilled air renewed with fragrance.

But last night, just words
and then numbness, raw as the wind
spilling into open spaces,
turning soil rigid.

This morning, I dialled and redialled your number.
Anxious. The ring, like an admonished child, crying
in an empty room. I imagined you seeking comfort
in someone else's arms. Hands, like mandrake,
taking root in each other's flesh.
Lips opening. Tongues like nightshade
dulling the hurt with sweet narcotic.

Tectonics

This kitchen is white
as the summer clothes I am wearing,
waiting to leave; as the blanket
of clouds that weigh down the sky.
The counter's edge is blunt,
hard-edged against the flesh
of finger you run along it
as your eyes stare straight ahead
through the window at rain
that quakes emerging leaves.

Only three feet between us.
But already oceans and continents fill this space
with the static that pounds in the background
of a telephone call from the other side of the planet.
Already we move in different worlds.
I under a sun igniting flamboyants,
you, in the shadow of foothills
that break the prairie's flow.

We could reach out. Say the things that lie
under our tongues. But
it would unleash such trembling —
tectonic plates rubbing
against the fragile lip of land.

Hiding Place

Our bodies seem weightless,
floating across this expanse of blue sheets.
We wish this would last forever.
The way children want
a summer's evening to go on and on,
everything running together:
sun lightening the dark notes of clouds,
wind giving voice to leaves.
But it won't.

In the darkening doorway,
our discarded clothes,
like parents, are frantic.
The arms of shirts, the cuffs of pants,
are mouths calling out.

Through the screen's mesh,
the father next door sounds annoyed;
his voice, a rubbing wheel,
demands the twins
quit their hiding place,
come out right now.

The Mirror

I stare down into the basin.
Water threaded with hairs
circles the drain.
I ease the tap, rinse the razor,
suddenly feel your chin nestle
my shoulder. One hand slips
into my bathrobe, probes a nipple,
the other the warmth of my thigh.
I look up into the mirror
and we appear two-headed,
siamese twins joined at the neck.
Your lips part in that quirky smile.

Inside, in memory's cavity
I still carry an image
of my wife. How she used to stand
behind me, watch me shave.
Her hair black and sleek,
her skin so white,
that laugh revealing the gap in her teeth.
Always when I had finished,
she would run a long thin finger
along the edge of my lip
as if trying to define its tension.
Or I would perch on the tub,
watch the soapy cloth take in
the hollow beneath her breasts.
Such small everyday intimate things
lovers share, like secrets,
nuances of their previous lives,
and yet still love unhesitantly
unafraid of the truth
they have turned from,
half-believing it can be undone
by pledging and bearing children.

But, sometimes there was that emptiness
I felt as a child looking down
an abandoned country well
and seeing my face floating
on its murky surface.
My likeness so far away
I could never be in touch with it.
Sometimes, from the recess of porch
I would watch men walk
along the path by our house
and feel such need for companionship,
a palm against my hand,
a bracket defining the space in between.
But I would return to our bed,
be taken into her arms,
into a caring embrace that brushed
the downy hairs on my chest
and tenderly led me,
released the anguish inside.
An anguish carved deeper by her illness,
that burst from my lips
as I watched her urn be covered with dirt.

And now here I am held by a man
still wanting an image
that has turned to dust,
and yet another, this reflection,
in a mirror I cannot seem to reach
even though it clearly gives back what I am.

Passport

I notice now it is in your hands
how this mask resembles my face
— concave shape, large forehead,
taut lips. I thought I was attracted
by its dark aesthetic,
how it would blend
with others you have collected.

Often you said you wanted
to lift off my masks
— the different ones
you think I wear
— the austere Celtic cleric,
the reserved stone face —
ones hiding the child
you conceive looming inside.

Once you watched me
shear stubble from my chin,
wanted to reach out,
as if the appearance in the mirror
were a goldfish floating below
the surface of the pond
in your parents' garden.

But it was never that easy.
Try as I might I could not be
what you wanted, could not give up
what I am. My face,
like yours, determined at conception,
shaped by those loved
and lost.

I offer you this,
a parting token — a passport
mask from Dahomey carved
by its bearer so he could leave
his ancestral village,
travel with this image
as protection. Take it
to be free to love whom you wish.
Hang it on your wall
among others you gather
as you explore faraway states.

In Dreams Begin Responsibilities

I push up from that altered state of sleep,
rush to the phone and my son's voice,
carried along clusters of fibre optics,
telling me he's arrived
safely in Florida.
I turn to the window.
A snow squall, like a meteor shower,
splinters in the streetlight.

One night last summer
in the wheat fields of northern Tanzania,
we climbed a boulder larger
than a two-storey house.
It was more difficult
than we had imagined.
Our hands against
the rough reality of stone
probed for holds to grasp onto,
our feet for wedges to support us
as we pushed further up and along.
At the top,
centuries of wind and rain
had etched a cleft in its curve,
two hemispheres of a brain.
Above us, in the inverted cup of sky
a plethora of stars so large
pressing down upon us.
He looked north
to find familiar constellations
— Andromeda, the Dipper —
and I south for the Cross.
We were so certain
being that close to the equator
both were possible.

We stood silent. I looked at how
his sixteen-year-old body shaped
the clothes he was wearing,
wondered at the galaxy of atoms
whirling inside of him.
At his age, I dreamt
of having a son I would raise on my own,
though I could never have predicted it this way.
I looked south again knowing
we could not read the pattern in the stars,
but must always continue to search.
Voyages, like arrows, are pointed,
our destination often our genesis,
leading us toward that we value most,
deeper and deeper into the heart.

DISCOVERING BUOYANCY

Footprints

Mother, what can I say?
Look how the garden is finished,
summer's abundance ragged,
yet the air so crisp and sharp,
the three maples in the laneway by this house,
brilliant as flames. Mother, look
at my hands at the edge
of this kitchen table where years ago
you broke wax seals, smoothed jam across bread
to feed your children, make us grow strong.

In my mind, the image of you always
snow furring the cuffs of your coat and boots
that you shook off with such determination
before entering the house to your children anxious
for news of our father in that overheated hospital room.
Each night, after dinner,
you set out to wait silently by his side.

Mother — there comes a time
when a child, or parent, must take the first steps,
form words that do not want to be shaped.
Love must be unconditional, a fire
we draw close to. I loved a woman.
Like you I walked draughty streets,
tedious corridors, sat and waited,
waited, watching disease waste her flare of life.
Mother, I can no longer disguise myself.
I must set myself free and go
forward, as my wife told me in her last week,
go forward. Mother,
I love men and have all my life.

At ten, I stood in a doorway,
peered through my handprint
on the frost thick pane,
saw your footprints across the porch,
down the stairs in the freshly fallen snow.

At the bottom you turned to me,
put fingers to your lips
before slipping them into a glove.
You stepped away into a circle of streetlight,
drawn toward the man you loved.

Stroke One, Stroke Two

Father, where did you go?
Each morning
your shoes buffed to gloss,
bow tie snapped on to starched collar,
the crease in your pants precise
as the minute, 6:45,
when you would come down the stairs,
take up from the newel post
your lunch, the folded hankie, the bicycle clips,
go out the door
and then, carefully balanced on your bike,
disappear around the corner.

Why as you grew older
did you refuse to acknowledge neighbours
who greeted you on the street,
invited you to stop for a drink and a chat
until, exasperated by the cold shoulder, they gave up?
Was it really only your heart?
The tightening around the chest,
the grasping for breath.
What was it you saw from beneath that plastic tent?
What were you saying through the mouth piece,
rasping as you spoke, as if trapped under water?
And in those last years,
for days not leaving your room,
couldn't bear the image of scars
etched on your jaw from the botched surgery
the doctors assured us removed all the tumours
and would prolong your life?

Father, I think I find you
each time I enter a room of glittering people
who can balance goblets of wine
and work the crowd with tales of far-flung travel.
I imagine you descending to the rowing club
beneath the bluffs of Rockcliffe Park,
into the circle of bronzed young men
in white flannels, pinpoint cotton, and boaters
their boasts of late parties at the Country Club,
their future in family firms.
Each time, I see you, in the scull,
your grip tightening, teeth grinding,
stroke one, stroke two,
pulling further out into the current,
away from them all,
away from the Centretown cold-water flat
your charwoman mother rented.

Discovering Buoyancy

This is where I first learned.
Each Monday of that winter. 1959.
We'd foot stomp paths through crusted banks,
wait at the Byron right-of-way.
The entire Grade Six class
at the back of a streetcar that glided,
as if skating across thin ice,
down Holland, along Somerset,
over the creaking bridge,
arched high as an eyebrow
above freight yards
where hoppers were laden with coal,
and then slid to a halt at Preston.

Once Sister Inez was left behind
in the glassed-in waiting room,
we'd shed our toques, mitts, duffle coats,
leggings and boots as if returning
to summer and the wading pool.
But here it was much deeper,
through lessons learned to let go of fear,
trust the body, though it could not touch the bottom,
discover buoyancy, the rhythmic beauty of arms and legs.

Today, I am alone. It is noon,
halfway between Christmas and New Year's,
the season of giving — the time of resolutions.
I plunge below the surface, my kick sending me down
so I can run my hands along the tiled floor.
All around the light, the water, such translucence,
illumination. I hold my breath
until panic pains my lungs,
explode up, grasping for air.
Today, I want to leave behind the ache for the dead,
for those who would not love me or whom I could not love.

I float on my back, scissor kick propelling me
toward the deep end. Now,
I want to love myself,
accept my sagging 42 year-old body,
my thinning, brittle hair.
I want to shed the guilt and sense of duty
as easily as my swimming suit,
walk unashamedly naked among the men,
smile at the desire that tingles my skin
like spray from the shower.
I want to get dressed, go out
and still be radiant, buoyant,
my identity crisp,
tangible as December air.

Poise

He enters the bus carrying the weight of the deluge.
It masses in his hair, knotted strands dripping
into the sodden winter coat that burdens his shoulders.
The storm runs after him, his mud-caked boots
trailing water as he presses down the aisle.

Once I saw him standing nude in a drawing.
The lines of his body so light they swept off the page,
the movement of a bird's wing disappearing against the sky.
The shading of hair suggested gorse;
ridges in his face the crowsfeet of half-hidden bushes.
And one fist nested in the crook of his groin.

Behind him the window crystallizes with raindrops.
The only hints of this other likeness —
the slight sway of his body as unheard notes
from the canary yellow Walkman float into his ears;
and his pants, the lilac of spring's evening sky.

The Ancient Course

A child yet a man, the teenager rocks back and forth.
His hands knot at his forehead, cup at his mouth.
He leans forward on the bench. I sit at the other end,
stare out at the darkness fallen across the river
making its way through this geological fault.
This river, when I was young, always swelled its banks
in spring. One year, it rose so high it drove
families from their homes and I came to watch
the torrent reclaim its ancient course.

The young man turns toward me, tries to smile.
Desperate to make a move but so afraid.
Not like these older men who saunter down the path.
These men with paunches and gold rings
who have pulled on muscle shirts and shorts
for this evening's walk, inclining their head
and slowing their stride before continuing on,
then veering to the left or right
along paths beaten into the grass.

The teenager abruptly stands, lurches before stopping
to face me full front. He spins on his heel, flees.
What could I have said? This pain of desire
will recede like water or drive him,
as the men who passed earlier,
into some woman's unsuspecting arms.
Each of us struggles to learn
to touch male flesh. Men have done this
since the beginning, as the river has,
swirling over shale,
hard as muscle, ribbed like a chest.

The White Room

This white room contradicts us —
the cotton duvet, the pillow shams,
the ruffle that skirts the bed.
These were designed for some bride,
who, after months of waiting,
can finally undo the clasps and stays
of her beaded dress and set herself free,
and a groom, sinewy and slim,
slipping off his cummerbund,
his studded wing-collar shirt.
Yet here we are, two middle-aged men,
sprawled across the queen-sized brass bed,
our bodies coarse
as the trunk of the maple
through the curve of bay window.
Our body hairs chalky as the snow
in the divides of that tree.

Once we both sought release in marriage.
We were young and sure that in loving women
we could refuse the truth, be completely restored
to an image our parents and books created.
Like this room, so tastefully appointed
with antiques retrieved from estate sales,
or from discards, refurbished, given new life.
Even from here, the fresh coat of varnish
does not hide the minute fissures
in the bowed legs of the chairs,
or the paint, the hairline cracks
at the edges of molding in the ceiling.

In the silvered mirror, our reflection
in this romantic room is ridiculous.
We are a little desperate perhaps
for the comfort of being held.
At our age, why care?
Our hands unfasten the rightful pleasure of skin.
Our mouths, not forming vows or even words,
only uttering sounds from deep within.

Beginning the Pattern

"It is so easy when you have the tools
— saw, hammer, drill and nails.
It's just a matter of taking
the tongue-in-groove boards
and laying them next to each other,
tapping them into place
across the sub-flooring
in any pattern,
being careful to leave some overlap."

You explain it to me so off-handedly
when I confess it is something I have never learned,
that my father was not skilled at such things
and I have inherited his ways.

His way, too, of being distant, unsure,
retreating into silence.
As if the tongue were nailed down.
The fear of reaching out.
The way a child, once burned, is leery
of the red-hot element that cooks the food
he needs to nourish his growing body;
is moulded to please his teachers,
the nuns and priests who would read each day
the life of a saint, driven
by love of God to endure
torture and pain rather than submit
to the pleasures of the flesh.

You hand me the boards and a hammer,
encourage me to begin a new pattern,
saying you will be close behind,
fastening it securely into place.

The Aftermath

My hands are immersed
in the sudsy water.
Against the matted hairs of my arm
float a bloated eye of tomato,
finger of skinless pepper, curl of spaghetti.
All week long on television,
the current affairs shows build
to the first anniversary of the Gulf War.
Over and over, serpents of fire
coil through night,
illuminate for an instant,
the gutted homes, like broken jaws,
the remnants of bodies
after the quick retreat.
How much can be absorbed
before such images leave a viewer
indifferent to everything?
To the terrified women, children and men,
desperate for shelter,
in Yugoslavia, Afghanistan, Mozambique,
countries cracked open like eggs.
Even to our own country
where bitter voices are served up,
filet of fish, toxic organs removed.

I look down at the aftermath
of this supper you have made me.
The first of many I hope.
I watch your reflection
in the window above the sink
as you rearrange leftovers in the fridge.
Its light silvers your hair.
You stand, then stop just inches away,
smile at me. How I want to lean back
against your chest,
into the cave of your arms.
But I hold back. I've learned love, too,
has a habit of reenacting familiar scenes.

Victims of war, we both have scars
that cannot be made to disappear
like the images on TV.

Across the lane, a man created an abstract mural
on the wall outside a summer kitchen
to welcome back his wife.
She had gone
to Africa seeking her roots.
The house has since been sold,
settlement in their divorce.
The hot tropic colours of the mural fade.
Was it an act of love? Perhaps a portent?
Like the war and its images
that rattle in my head.
The food that clots
as the sinks drain.

Dioscuri

Slightly out of breath
I mount these wide slate stairs,
edged with white marble,
that are cut steeply into the side
of Capitoline Hill where Michelangelo created
the Piazza del Campidoglio,
set two facing palaces
at slightly different angles
to create an illusion,
make the piazza seem larger than it is.

I rest momentarily, look up, and there
at the entrance, the naked marble bodies
of Castor and Pollux gaze out
over the city, as if lost in thought.
Even after all these centuries
of exposure to wind and rain and
more lately exhaust
from billions of buzzing cars,
they are still beautiful,
their muscles firm,
a celebration of virility.

On the day I left, you looked out
over my garden, its first tender shoots emerging.
After winter and days of chilling rain,
the mulch of straw was beaten and sodden.
You turned, leaned against the windowframe.
I was filled with such desire.
"Will spring ever come?" Then you smiled.
The curve of your mouth soft and full
as the umbrella pine that leans
against the balustrade. Your jeans blue
as the Roman sky that drapes against the flesh
of these two statues.

Released Through Stone

Santa Catharina. Ora pro nobis.
Santa Anna. Pray for us.
In the enclave at the front
of Basilica San Clemente
a nun's arms are flung wide,
a bird attempting flight,
as in a quintocento painting of a mystic
suspended in mid-air.
Her head tilted back,
eyes fixed on the gold mosaic,
above the altar, ablaze
with twilight sun streaming
into the chapel of the Virgin.
Santa Maria. Santa Cecilia.
Singsong of her voice grows stronger,
echoes against the walls.

I turn away, turn down
a stairwell, past the church
underneath with faded frescoes,
down to the cavern below
gouged from the earth
a millennium before,
through passageways
where the sound of water
fills the chamber.
I stop, run my hand over
a marble fragment
- muscled arm and shoulder,
cool as sleeping flesh.
Here there are only broken shards
of bone, cracked sarcophagus,
the smell of soil sweet as ripe fruit,
lichen, green as velvet,
on the seeping walls.

I stop, entranced by a barred chamber.
In a niche the torso
of Mirhri, the Persian sun god,

rises against the dark brown earth.
His amorphic shape
one with my adolescent dreams
which I would reach out to touch,
only to waken into darkness.
A masculine form still
puzzling, the image
behind my shut eyes
when longing and desire
fill my solitary bed,
there even when I hold
another man in my arms.

Here in this grotto,
there is no need for invocation,
or denial.
This icon is an idol
willed into being by the sheer force
of a unknown sculptor's hands,
the turn of its straining thighs,
the thrust of the primal
released through stone.

Restoration

So wondrous. Up here
in this vault of attic. My head
over the edge of your bed,
blood pounding in my ears.
Through the window, as if a fresco,
late winter sky blue
and plump clouds hovering
against the coarse arms of two maples,
their buds rough fingers pointing,
reaching out. Taproot of icicle
drips to the ground, glazes the surface
of this week's sudden snow.

But in here.
Your mouth moving up and down
the shank of my cock
glistening with saliva.
The weight of one palm
against the cavity of my chest,
which emptied, is frantic for breath.
Your other hand arcing through the air,
its thick index finger
suspended above mine.

Such sensation. Such wanting.
As if being reborn. New beginning.
And spinning. As when head thrown back,
I stared up at the ceiling of the Sistine Chapel.
Its restoration unleashing lush pastels
in Michelangelo's celebration of the body.
Not the Adam shaped out of dust,
but ample-fleshed, inclined,
compelling his maker's touch.

Travelling Alone

Take it, you insisted.
Your Michelin guide to ancient Rome.
Flipping open the pages carefully,
the spine broken from being well-thumbed,
you said the best ruins are the ones
you marked. Your hand lingered on mine
as I took the book, tucked it
carefully in my luggage,
smiling, imagining one day we might travel
as lovers.

Once off the plane, the taxi hurtled me
through the quiet roadways,
early morning shadows dark as priests in cassocks.
I checked into the hotel, unpacked the guide, set out.
It took my breath away,
the Coliseum, there, at the end of the street,
a broken honeycomb through which the sun poured.
You, an artist, were right.
The light here beautiful, exquisite as saffron.
From some cavern inside, pilgrims sang the *Te Deum*,
their voices careened among the stones,
exposed as if the venerated corpse of a martyr.

Then on to St. Peter-in-Chains. This you gave three stars.
It was dark and damp. Scaffolding everywhere
as if it were about to collapse on itself.
But off to the right, the unfinished tomb of Pope Julius,
Michelangelo's Moses. A tourist clunked a coin into the meter.
The light against the sculpted muscled arms a shimmer of water.
I thought of you stepping out of the shower
after we had made love. You bent to the bed,
a pool of drops gathered on my chest.
For the first time, I felt the isolation
of the tourist travelling alone. Fatigue made me skittish.
I turned back to the hotel where, although only noon,
I fell into the dead of sleep.

All week long, each day after work,
your choices guided me into basilicas,
down the Spanish Steps, through the Terme di Caracalla,
but also to less-travelled sites.
Feeling out-of-place,
among the elegant Italian men you raved about.
I thought about you and me, so similar,
craving beauty everywhere. Soothing the pain.
All our life walking among the remnants
of our past, rendering, transforming them,
the way floodlights at night
accented the monuments,
gave them surrealistic splendour.

By mid-week, I imagined us in bed once again,
waking from the brief drowse men fall into
after sex, comparing insights, impressions.
But although the plane brought me closer,
you withdrew, kept retreating,
always a last minute change of plans.
I sought guidance, explanations,
confused by your tactics, your cryptic signs.

Now I willingly wander
among the monuments of my own city.
I stare up at the flank of bronze soldiers
in the arch of the War Memorial.
The sculptor has them advancing,
a battalion of heroic men
marching through the eye of a needle.
I, too, have finally chosen to pass through.
High above, on the arc of granite,
winged Peace and Freedom hold up
a torch and laurel to the open sky.

The Pool

For hours these two Englishwomen
have sat in the dark shade
of the overhang and said not a word.
Cotton floral print smocks cover
thick set legs and bellies that sag with age.
Plain hands folded across plump purses.
One older; the other, her image
some thirty years ago.
Mother and daughter perhaps who,
having lived together for so long,
endure their relationship of warmth
and silence as the others here give themselves
to the sun in the ritual of tanning.

With his greying curls and thickening build,
this Italian could be David
had Michelangelo waited another twenty years.
His confident stride circles the patio that girds
the pool, pauses in front of the German girls
who sit round a table, their red lips
sipping tropical drinks.
His stomach contracts, the string of his
bikini bathing suit draws tighter,
the cloth against his scrotum shear as onion skin.
Arms and legs begin to stretch, thrust;
his body jackknives into the pool.
A gurgle of sounds applaud as straws
draw the last of the amber liquid
into the hollows of mouth.

The American, in the dark glasses
and trim moustache, crisscrosses the pool.
His scissorkick below the water
is hidden by sunlight that coats the surface.
At his table, a young Thai, his face
obscured behind a glass of Coke.
A waiter asks him if he wants anything else.
His eyes look down. In his fingers
a hotel matchbook flips open.

The Frenchwoman's wax treatment
allows the sun to caress
the inside of her slim thighs
barely covered by black cloth.
The straps of her top undone,
no unsightly white line will mar
the effect of her strapless silk dress
she tells her husband she bought
this morning for tonight's formal dinner.
Not to be outdone, he spreads
the lotion carefully on his face, his body,
a balance sheet highlighting
his assets, the bottom line.
The thick gold bracelet
around his wrist inlaid with sun.
The Asian Wall Street Journal waits
patiently at his feet.

And you and I, having left behind
in separate rooms our business clothes,
also lounge at the edge.
It is the first time
we've seen each other this way.
I steal glimpses of the sapphire trunks
that hug your tensed body;
you, the flesh-toned briefs
I bought on a whim and now regret.
Slowly our conversation navigates
around being in our forties
and the turbulence caused by the need
for companionship and always
the dark undertow of love.
We suddenly grow silent, aware perhaps
that we've gone too far.
You turn on your stomach taking full
advantage of the hot rays of the setting sun.
I, always cautious, retreat,
wade into the chill
waters of the overcrowded pool.

The Narrow Channel

You stand at a distance,
your hands behind your back
as you watch the foreign barge
approach the narrow channel,
withdraw from Durban's harbour.
Your hands folded into one another,
our bodies this morning when we awoke.
Such elegant hands that drew from keys
music shaped at the dawn
of this century
to ears unaccustomed
to such sounds.

At the left of the pier,
the strong grips of young males
cast fine lines into the waves,
hoping for the big catch
that will provide tomorrow's sustenance.
To the right, in the curve
of the city's golden shore,
the robust fingers of men in wetsuits
lose control of their wind surfers,
their bodies propelled into the spray.

This morning I took you into my mouth
— your throbbing, pulsing flesh —
and tasted salt, the fishy tang of seed.
It woke in me such longing to speak
of the need for sex, but more,
my fear of rejection.
To tell you I once loved a man
of the cloth who pursued me cunningly,
and once he had me
spurned me, leaving this legacy.

You watch the barge move
slowly toward the open sea
tell me how the channel had to be dug,
scoops of sand and rock
dredged up, finally set free.

My eyes survey the prow of the ship,
its bulk driving the water apart.

Clair de Lune

Lying alone against white sheets
in Bloemfontein, Afrikaans country.
Through the hotel window,
the new moon in the old moon's arms.
And you, beyond the Drakensberg,
far away on the tropic coast
where you were born into splendour.

For four days your life unfolded,
through album after album,
black and white photos of bright young men
you courted, who pursued you
in Africa, Europe and Asia
as you toured, drawing waltzes, sonatas
from the ivory and ebony of grand pianos
to greater and greater acclaim.

Now eighty-one, saddened by the ridged image
the mirror gives back to you
and questioning why I make love
to you, yet never stopping
your knurled fingers from running
along the curve of my thigh,
into the thicket of pubis.

You permitted me your stories.
As we lay on our sides
the younger you rose to the surface,
the skin of a dried peach
still so sweet to the taste,
an impression imprinting itself
on photographic paper.

Your laughter was as easy
as the surf beating Durban's golden shore,
certain as your fingers against my skin,
the keys when you played Debussy's
Clair de Lune, a farewell gesture.

Stills of Your Life

One year and the taste still vivid.
The air pungent with sea,
dampness so pervasive
it stained walls,
mildewed sheet music
spread out across your grand piano.
I can still hear
the endless vibrations of cars
swooshing along the arterial, or,
in those quiet moments at night,
fronds of palms beating
against the barred bedroom window,
regular as hearts
in cavities of chests.

In front of me, here in this frozen country,
stills of your life -
London 1938 - profile, smooth luminous skin;
Durban 1950 - dark cravat at your throat,
arm along the keyboard,
looking off toward the source of light;
Sydney 1979 - open collar, soft folds
in flesh of your throat, the corners of your eyes,
such a flash of smile;
then an informal one, just a snapshot,
your favourite - your 80th birthday,
portrait of the laughing cavalier you called it.

I sit here alone,
as I so often do,
photos across my bed, wanting
a letter on that blue paper
you always write you detest.
But for me, it is the ocean
that day we walked along the curl of bay,
our bodies electric with desire;
the cloudless sky behind your head
that first time you reached out,
your lips dry against mine.

Incarnation

How exotic, these images your fingers turn,
the book lying open above your crotch.

In this one, the sky black with monsoon clouds,
a shaft of sun gilds a temple in the hills of Kaimur.

In the next, a group of men wash, their dhotis,
wet with the water of the Ganges, almost transparent,
skin of onion cradling flesh.

I watch your fingertip, as it touches each image
as if its brush transports you there
to your childhood land, heals
the anguish distance has created,
which I catch in the breath.

A statue fully dressed, with long flowing hair,
nestles against the tensed muscles of the devout.

All I can do is watch your hand,
the colour of the Indian tea
you've made me, which I hold.
Dark hairs thread across knuckles
as your fingers lengthen,
turn the pages longingly
then rest beneath the edge of cover,
against my thigh.

Carved into sandstone, a deity
copulates, his mouth ajar.

You run a finger along this embodiment
carved long ago by a sculptor.

All this is foreign to me — these myths
you intuitively understand. In mine,
it is humans not god that covet,
but I believe in this presence of body,
desire, incarnation of image and thought.

Your hand descends once more.

A page flips open,
three women pull red saris
across their faces,
turn away.

Purification

You have flipped many pages,
yet the image still burns my eyes
this holy man —
mask of face, grizzled, haired,
eyes seized with delirium.

But the mouth, his mouth,
embedded with hooks
as if he were a fish lugged out
of its element, as if
cross-stitched
to stop his breathing,
speaking of his vision,
from the depths of pain.

For so many years, in the morning
a razor severed the dark grains
on my chin, left me astonished
at the taut lines gathered
at the edge of my lips,
set like strata of limestone
heaved to the surface
centuries after the earth's furnace
broiled and seared the debris.

I had been taught to believe
in Plato's Cave of Illusion,
the prisoners' struggle up the path
to its mouth, desperate to look upon the sun,
and St. John of the Cross, consumed by guilt
and sin, who kept his body raw with sores.

And now this man's face, racked with bliss,
though his mouth is pierced and suffering,
his lips mirroring
my final surrender,
final peace.

Linguistics

Your apartment is shadowed by moonlight
falling through slats of venetian blind.

In the corner, the green light of the CD
pulses, the rhythm of a vein under skin.

The music, in a language I can't comprehend,
though I recognize melancholic complaint.

Pages of a dictionary in my lap fall to each side.
You, in the kitchen concocting tea.

On the right, the Urdu script floats,
each shape a curlicue, a ribbon in space.

On the left, Hindi links each sound
fixes the word rigidly in place.

These phrases I can't even enunciate
though my mouth wants to take them in

have my tongue make them mine,
the way tea once ingested is part of the body.

The way the scuff of your shoes across the floor,
the ring of spoon against lip of cup

conjures your presence in the other room,
slight torso pressed against kitchen counter.

When you return to this room, mugs in hand,
we will begin to speak, each in his own way.

Your English clipped yet soft with cadence,
the sound of tropic rain on a roof.

Mine, hard-edged as the pre-Cambrian shield,
scarred by the passing of time.

Our intentions expressed by the movements we choose.
Your finger lingering after the cup is offered.

My grip tightening around the curved stem
careful so the infusion will not spill, scald.

You will sit at the far end of the couch,
I will remain here close to the lamp,

disparate as North and South,
the societies through which we speak.

Despite how we have been schooled to pronounce,
rules are not constant, our bodies

can shift symbols, become the values
our throats will decode.

Crossing Over

The sun warm on my face
as I cross over the Glen Road bridge.
Below, in the ravine cutting apart
the land mass north of Bloor, willows
among the steelwool of trees, are already yellow;
the air flits with robins and blackbirds
which manoeuvre down from branches in search of worms.

I step off the curb, pass Beaumont Road.
Timothy Findley's **Headhunter** tucked under my arm.
In it, an amber autumn fog holds the city captive,
a frustrated woman in a white limousine
brings lovers deeper into her, disease
is spread by starlings
and officials exterminate them.
Today, however, in the real world,
couples throw open windows,
rake lawns, pull back the damp mush of leaves
to give light to first tender shoots.

Today in your highrise apartment,
you move about tidying the shambles
we made of your bed.
My mouth still savours the taste
of your cock, my lips the throb
of blood in the vein of its shaft.
My ears hear the soft cries you made,
ice breaking apart in late winter.
I, too, have broken apart.
Freed myself, at least for a night,
from the isolation self-doubt imposes,
the way earth now lets go of frost,
holds, once again, promise.

Near Rosedale United
many of those with rakes along these streets
carefully avoid tearing buds emerging
by their houses' foundations, condemn
what we did through the night.

God's wrath evidenced by the deaths
of so many men. They would deny
both you and me. But in the real world,
in this city alone,
in tens of thousands of bedrooms,
men and women like us cross
over the expanse of sheets.
Their mouths open to flesh
that tastes of who they are.

Manhood

Is this really a symbol of power?
This flesh and blood you take in your hand
and stroke so gently
my mind is charged:
a bow drawn to the point of release;
a kite somersaulting in the air,
tethered to earth by a fist.

The pleasure unleashed in me
I have craved all my life,
was taught to fear it
by teachers and friends who have never known
this dark forge of desire;
but mostly by myself, who defined being a man
along precise lines of conduct,
who, having tasted it briefly,
withdrew so as not to be scorched,
though its burn was indelible,
like the whorl of birthmark
staining my thigh.

The vibration of your palm against my skin
is a circle calibrating the focus.
My lips round, descend toward you.
Through them you enter, thrust.
I am truly alive,
know what it is to be male,
to hold and be held by a man,
not through conquest but sharing,
rich imaginings rising up from
the body's core, seismic,
flesh against flesh
rocking this divide of sheets.

Subversion

As a young boy I loved
a priest who hid
his longing for male flesh,
sought it in the company of altar servers.
His desire burning like a coal inside a censer,
which, once doused with myrrh, smouldered,
the air suddenly acrid.

You advise me not to use words
— cock, crotch, cum —
that my poems are complex, layered
and such words only get in the way,
are voyeuristic, too explicit,
far too political.

Should songs of love be only
ambiguous, discrete,
shadows falling across bushes,
or with curtains drawn
masking interior scenes?

For years, I said nothing,
though I could not deny
the voice that spoke, if only inside,
longing for hands,
the thrill of fingers at waistbands,
anticipation of wet mouth against flesh.

And it would not be quiet
even when I pierced my skin
with pins, conjuring
the image of a gaunt saint
in a desert cave.

Even for a child, sex
can be pleasurable,
what is not
is the lesson
that grown-up words
are treacherous,
double-headed coins,
— on one side, the mouth begs for release;
on the other, it cries shame.

A child shapes his world
by what he experiences,
learns to be cunning,
risks uttering certain phrases
even knowing there will be
the tang of soap in his mouth,
a slap leaving
a handprint across his cheek.

By trial and error, language is mastered,
the child subverted becomes an adult
who confides only in private
and when disabled by truth.

Some poems about love dare
to speak of the body,
unafraid of its dangers.